Pickle Juice: The Fluid Motion Factor for Pickleball

Play freer. Play lighter. Play in flow.

Cover design: Paul Stokstad
Interior design: Paul Stokstad

ISBN: 979-8-9943781-1-3 (paperback)
Library of Congress Control Number: 2025927997
First paperback edition: January, 2026

Printed in the United States of America

Publisher Locations:
Fairfield, Iowa and Vero Beach, Florida

For information, contact:
paul@stokstad.com

Disclaimer

The information in this book is offered for educational and entertainment purposes only. It reflects the authors' opinions and experiences as players, observers, and coaches of pickleball and related mind/body practices.

Pickle Juice is not a substitute for professional medical advice, diagnosis, or treatment. Playing pickleball and engaging in any physical or mental training described in this book involves inherent risks, including the risk of injury. Before beginning or changing any exercise, training program, or competitive activity, you should consult with a physician or other qualified health-care professional to determine what is safe and appropriate for you.

The authors and publishers make no guarantees about specific performance results, competitive outcomes, or

Table of Contents

Note to the Reader

We chose Pickle Juice as a title because it carries the humor, energy, and flavor of the game itself. It's memorable, playful, and true to the spirit of flow. Inside these pages, you'll see the Fluid Motion Factor system at work, but the juice is what keeps it alive.

This book is the result of conversations between two friends, two teachers, and countless hours on court.

Steven brought the Fluid Motion Factor system, honed over decades of teaching athletes at the highest level. Paul brought a poet's ear, a player's heart, and the joy of exploring what it means to live in flow.

What you'll find here is not a manual to be memorized, but a companion to your play. Read it, reflect on it, try the cues, and return to it as your game evolves. The Fluid Motion Factor is not a trick or a shortcut — it's a way of being present.

We invite you to enter the game with us.

— Steven Yellin and Paul Stokstad

Why Pickle Juice?

It's a fun title, but there's more in the name than it may seem at first glance. We looked at many names, such as "Inner Pickle" but that's too much like the Gallwey tennis book. "Silent Pickle" would be a gratifying idea for sound sensitive types who are driven crazy by pickleball games going on at all hours of the day in their neighborhood (if only our book would fix that). Then there was "Zen Pickle" but that comes with all the baggage of the monastery and there's the temptation to push the analogy of zen to the limit and lose sight of pickleball itself.

And the other element has to do with dynamism, because even though we are going to talk a lot about inner states, all of those other titles are kind of passive, and we don't want to lose sight of the dynamism and excitement of playing your best in a game enhanced by the Fluid Motion Factor, which is deeply quiet while being dynamically effective.

You will really enjoy yourself, you will be energized, laser-focused, and you will be high-fiving, laughing, and celebrating. You will be juiced, and in a good way.

So, Pickle Juice.

But there's more, considering two kinds of players:

The No Juice Player

The no Pickle Juice player is not all bad. And that's a good thing, because they are everywhere. As a matter of fact, they are often admired and emulated. Describing this seems almost unnecessary, because it is so common as to be expected. They look good: they are intense, deeply competitive, and focused on every point. They want to win in a big way. They are extremely alert. They care about the final score, and watch line calls with intensity, ready to argue one way or another. They are exalted and cheer for any great shot by themselves or their team and celebrate errors or mistakes by their opponents. On the downside, they are bitterly disappointed with mistakes by themselves or their partner. Sometimes that results in comments or even advice to their partner. After they miss a ball, they analyze what went wrong and commit to doing better next time. They carry all those self-commitments around like post-it notes in their mind, hoping that they will recall those yellow comments on demand. Sometimes they do, and sometimes they don't, which can result in even more intense self-recrimination.

The Pickle Juice Player

The Pickle Juice player might as well be on another planet. They are cultivating presence, not wins. They know that their body can hit great, effective shots without supervision, and so they cultivate a situation that gets out of the way, by quieting mental noise and control. When they miss a shot, they know what went wrong in a technical sense, but they don't obsess over that. They are more concerned with whether they got pulled out of what we will be describing as the Fluid Motion Factor. They simply can't get mad at themselves, because they are stepping out of being in-charge of what is happening, by letting the body play with internal support, rather than urgent, clumsy, mentally shouted directions.

A different player indeed. Rare, but amazing. And amazingly effective.

Why Pickleball?

Before we explain the Fluid Motion Factor in detail, let's consider why something that creates what is sometimes referred to as a "zone" experience, that is, a situation of unrushed inner calm where all your play seems effortless and highly effective, might go so well with pickleball. A shorter way of saying that would be "Why is Pickle Juice so good for Pickle?" (Pickle is the affectionate short name for pickleball.)

Let's start by mentioning the timing issue. Pickleball does not come with the comparatively leisurely between-shot timeframes of tennis. The contrast with golf is unimaginably distinct. You might buy and sell whole companies waiting for someone to tee off or putt. It has certainly happened. In addition, pickleball requires going from zero to 60 in a microsecond, and often back to near zero again. And the reason for that can be discerned from one aspect of pickleball: the kitchen. The decision to distance players seven feet away from the net with a no-volley zone (the kitchen) is what made pickleball into a fascinating, hyper-fast and then slow, intricate, and tactical game.

Yes, you can slam the ball. Yes, you can hit a dominant overhead (though it often comes back). But you must also have the soft game that allows you to drop a third shot at your opponent's feet and join them at the kitchen line.

Pickleball switches from force to delicacy in an instant. Watching a professional pickleball match you don't only see powerful dominance. You see tactical moves, intricate placements interspersed with quick volleys, lobs, powerful overheads, counterpunches back into the kitchen, followed by more delicate tactical dinks, until someone misses or hits the ball too high and then it is smashed, angled, or dropped out of reach.

All of this responds wonderfully to Fluid Motion Factor-enhanced play. Steven advises that the mind should slow down during the point. Let's consider how radical that statement is, and how rarely that is ever an athlete's experience.

In pickleball you can easily get into a shootout at the kitchen line where, unless someone resets the ball as a dink, no one has any control over the end of the point. It's anyone's ball. Everyone is on high alert and as the ball is hit faster, all four minds are accelerating. It's a crapshoot at that point and anyone could win or lose.

Just imagine being able to slow that down and find more time to adjust in that frenzy.

Who do we love in pickleball? Ben Johns, who has all the power you need, but also a magic shot where he runs past the ball to the kitchen line and hits the ball from behind him as a perfect dink, finishing three feet closer to the line than he would otherwise have been.

Who do we love in tennis? Carlos Alcaraz, who hits with power and precision, but two points before winning $8 million at the US Open wins a point with a nonchalant dropshot. Total freedom and playfulness. Yes, we want to win, but we win more with balance, a sense of play, and freedom.

Who has it in basketball? Steph Curry, and now Caitlin Clark, stepping back and demonstrating their calm, deep connection, ball to basket.

And what about Muhammad Ali, floating like a butterfly, stinging like a bee?

It's a coexistence of opposite values. Dynamic action. Deep silence. Focus and freedom.

Pickle Juice. Especially good for pickleball.

Zero, Zero, Start – The When, Where, What, and How of Fluid Motion

The foundation of this book is the Fluid Motion Factor (FMF) program developed by Steven and taught to Paul in reference to both tennis and pickleball. The FMF is a revolutionary mental training program that has been taught in 12 sports, including seven professional sports. It is revolutionary, because although it is a mental program, it is not based on any aspect of sports psychology but rather on a set of neurophysiological processes in the brain itself. All sports are about motion, so let's first understand the neurophysiological origin of motion.

To initiate a motion, any motion, whether it be walking across the street or hitting a pickleball, you must generate an intention, an electrical signal in the brain, or the feet won't move and the arms won't swing. Though there are numerous physiological steps involved in this process, let's talk about two of the principles involved in producing fluid motion: the pre-frontal cortex (PFC) and the motor system.

The PFC, also known as the CEO of the brain, is the discriminating intellect and oversees all processes in the brain. When you are thinking, it is the PFC that is doing the thinking. Like a real CEO, it wants to micromanage any motion you produce, but that's not good a thing because we all know the results when you start over-thinking out there, and they're not good.

When you want to produce a motion, you generate a signal and the ideal scenario is that this signal instantaneously travels to the motor system and it is the motor system that communicates with the body to produce the motion that you want.

But when the PFC goes online, which means you are thinking too much, that signal is ever-so-slightly interrupted in moving to the motor system. Then in the middle of the motion, the body is looking for direction, but there are too many processes going on in that brain of yours and so the bulkier, core levels of the muscles dominate. Then, a less-than-fluid motion is produced because there is simply not enough intelligence flowing and the body does not know exactly what to do. Of course this is all happening in milliseconds, but the sequence of the signal getting interrupted or not happens on every shot.

When the signal moves to the motor system seamlessly, which obviously is the ideal scenario, we call that process the Fluid Motion Factor. It is neither Steven's nor Paul's process. It is a universal neurophysiological phenomenon that occurs when any athlete in any sport produces a fluid motion. This is why the program has been taught in multiple sports. Regardless of what motion is being produced, the processes that produced that motion are identical. The only problem is that pickleball players (and virtually every athlete in every sport) don't know when during a point they will access the Fluid Motion Factor or how to access it on the next point, and when it leaves, where to look to get it back. This book will teach you how to access this subtle process by design, rather than wishing and hoping it shows up by chance.

What makes Fluid Motion so slippery is that this highly valued process arrives only when you stop chasing it. You can't brute force your way in. The prefrontal cortex, or PFC — that chatterbox narrator in your head — wants to command, direct, critique. It tries to drive the bus. But in flow, the PFC takes the back seat, letting deeper systems of the brain and body handle the ride. We'll go into detail on the PFC and the other, deeper, Fluid Motion-flavored systems soon, but for now, just consider that this book is about clearing the way for these systems to take the wheel on every shot. Not through mystical spells or mechanical drills, but by learning how to stop interfering.

We'll explain how Fluid Motion is your body's natural intelligence, operating without the drag of self-consciousness. It's not just a state of peak performance; it's a state of freedom. Think of it this way: Fluid Motion is less about doing more, and more about getting out of your own way.

The origin of the knowledge in this book is an experience that Steven had some years back (quite a few now) in an intrasquad challenge match when he was a senior playing #1 singles on the University of Pennsylvania tennis team. Steven had a stellar junior career, winning the Florida High School singles championship, and also as a member of the championship high school team. He went on to have a solid career on UPenn's tennis team. But after being on the All-Ivy team as a sophomore, he started to get burned out in the game and the joy of playing started to dissipate almost after every match.

But then one day the magic showed up. Big time. He had a life-changing experience that led him on a path that now has the potential to revolutionize how sports are played and taught. While competing against a fellow Penn player, he slipped into that extraordinary space where any sport becomes effortless and ridiculously simple and effective. He simply played the best tennis of his life. His movement, his racquet control, his balance, his shot selection, his consistency (virtually no unforced errors), his service percentage, his level of freedom; everything was on another level.

At the end of the match he felt as if he had received a gift from the tennis gods above and knew his life had changed then and there because sports were such a central part of his life. He sat down afterwards and literally could not move for ten minutes. Not only was this the most extraordinary tennis match he ever played, it was also the most extraordinary experience he'd ever had in his life. It was a deeply moving spiritual experience that transcended the normal parameters of space and time and during it he felt he was outside his body witnessing a higher intelligence guiding his shots.

If someone watched him play that match and knew his game, they would say how smooth and fluid everything looked, but he knew that was a by-product of something that had occurred way below the radar and he wanted to understand the cause. He had to understand what precipitated it, so he was on it 24/7. Why? He had played so many matches against so many players at so many venues, why did this experience show up today and not last week or last year? After several days of examining, from every conceivable angle, he had a Eureka insight. It was like a lightning bolt had struck and gave him the knowledge that would change his life.

Here's the answer in terms of pickleball.

When you are reading a book and someone asks you what's the main point you usually must think about it for a while and come up with something. But we are going to save you all that trouble by coming right out and telling you what it is in advance and explain why Steven had his remarkable zone experience. Not only that, we're letting you know that if you just get clear on this one thing you will have done most of the heavy lifting that reading this book requires.

So, here it is.

When you watch a pickleball match what do you see? Well, it's obvious. Someone hits a shot and then another person hits a shot, and this continues until the point is won.

But we're not done, not by a wide-angled kitchen shot.

If you want to see the whole picture, there is something else going on. After you hit a shot, you must wait to hit another shot. Then your opponent hits a shot, and they must wait to hit a shot. So, just for a moment, if we shift our attention from the person hitting the pickleball to the person waiting for it, we could, just for discussion purposes, redefine pickleball not as a series of shots, but as a series of "waitings" — a series of gaps.

People naturally think of pickleball as a series of motions or a series of shots. But we, being the radical, wrong way — or maybe innovative — folks we are, prefer to define pickleball as a series of gaps.

And as it turns out (here it comes, the central point of this, our central point section), the quality of the gap will always determine the quality of the shot.

We'll say it again. **The quality of the gap will always determine the quality of the shot.**

Everything that we say in this book is about making sure that the quality of the gap is as pure and free as possible. If there is an imbalance in how you are waiting in the gap, that imbalance will show up in the shot.

We define imbalance in terms of how you are experiencing time. It's the experience of time that controls the muscles. When there is the slightest over-anticipation of an event that has not occurred, even if that event will happen in a millisecond, then the experience of time gets distorted and there is not enough intelligence flowing from the mind into the body which in terms affects all aspects of the shot; timing, balance, paddle position, contact point, shot selection, follow-through.

Did we leave anything out? (Yes, dinks, but you get the point.)

When you are experiencing time normally, meaning you are not in the slightest over-anticipating the shot, you are drinking the Juice! Lots of it. Then the intelligence is flowing into your body like a car on the autobahn doing 150 MPH (or 241 KPH, since you are in Germany).

In that situation the game starts to slow down and flow, you are moving gracefully and quickly, your reaction time is excellent, your timing is spot on, all good is occurring.

You have probably experienced the gap correctly and incorrectly hundreds, if not thousands of times when you played. Here, we're going for the good stuff, repeatedly.

When Steven had his first Fluid Motion experience, he had never experienced the gap in such a pure form. There wasn't the slightest over-anticipation of the shot, and he was completely in the present, even as he was taking the racquet back and moving it forward. And consequently, his shots were smooth, powerful, and effortless.

He then realized that what separated him from the top 20 players in the country was they had this correct experience of the gap more consistently. This experience led him to formulate a remarkable insight applicable to every sport, which is, as we have indicated, that the quality of the space before you initiate a motion will determine the quality of the motion.

It is like you are creating a seed for the motion in the gap and if you create a good seed (defined by the experience of time), the motion will unfold successfully. But the opposite also applies. If time gets distorted in the gap, time will be distorted during the motion, and the results usually do not turn out well. By the time the motion starts, it's usually too late to adjust — the ship has left the port.

But how can we have the correct experience of the gap more often?

Let's say it's a bright and cheery pickle morning and you are returning a serve, and just about every serve you return is excellent, deep in the court, challenging, keeping them back while you politely but swiftly make your way to the kitchen line. Smooth, easy, simple, effective.

But that afternoon, you are playing a tournament match against someone you really want to beat.

They serve more slowly than the person you were practicing against in the morning, but those solid and effective returns you had in the morning have left the building and are apparently lunching on crumpets and tea. Why?

Granted, it was a practice match in the morning, and everyone is going to be looser in a friendly pickup game than in a tournament match. But how are we defining looser?

Even with the quick motion of a pickleball serve, there is a split second between the time when the ball leaves the hand and when it's hit. And there is an even longer gap before that serve gets to you. The difference in returns between your morning session and your afternoon session was how you experienced those gaps. In the morning session, you experienced time normally, so the intelligence was flowing beautifully into the body. In the afternoon match the result of you wanting to play well, wanting to win, not wanting to lose, wanting to hit winning shots, was that the experience of time was distorted in the gap. There was not sufficient intelligence flowing into the body.

This paradigm shift, such that you mentally reframe pickleball as a series of gaps rather than as a series of shots, will change your game. From this perspective you will not really be playing against your opponents, but rather playing to see where you are, how you are functioning in the gap.

This leads to the second paradigm shift: as soon as you feel you are playing against the other person, you have already lost. And that will be because you will be out of the gap, out of the focus on the gap experience.

We modestly suggest that this is a mind-shifting, universe-exploding, reality-bending understanding that will give you your best chance of having those magical PB games which you will remember forever.

As soon as you feel it's me against you or us against them, on every shot you will connect a subtle, but real umbilical cord to your opponents. You will always be in the future, distorting time and be at the mercy of what they are doing. You will not be the captain of your own ship. You will be thinking "What are they going to do on this shot?," "What am I going to do if they hit it there or over there." You're always guessing and second-guessing. Trapped.

But as soon as you see your sport as a series of gaps, you stop generating umbilical cords, you start living totally in the present, you have full unfettered attention to every ball, and your mind and body will be consciously thanking you for having read this book and setting you free from the old style of competition and leading it into the new world of your best possible pickleball. You will really enjoy yourself; you will be energized, laser-focused, and you will be high-fiving, laughing and celebrating. You will be juiced, and in a good way. Pickle Juiced.

Just to show you that fluid motion is produced identically in all sports, if you sat down with a hundred athletes from different sports and asked them how they felt when playing their best, you could probably divide their responses into three categories. See if you can relate to these three.

Category 1:

Time slows down. During a motion, you feel you have all the time in the world. For instance, you are at the beginning of your shot, and it feels like you have all the time in the world before you start your hit. The experience of time is controlled by neurons in the PFC and neurons in the motor system. When the PFC goes online the neurons in the PFC will overshadow the neurons in the motor system and you will experience time moving quickly. No one wins 11-0, walks off the court and says time was rushed out there. What do they say? What do you say? Time slowed down.

Category 2:

It felt like you were not thinking too much. The mind felt very quiet and you didn't remember much about what you did during the shots or even during the match. Everything felt automatic and timeless. The PFC is the intellect and when it goes online you will remember every detail. After an easy win, no one walks off the court and says they were thinking a lot during the match. They will probably say they were not thinking much at all.

Some stories from some other sports highlight this point.

This is a quote from an interview with Tiger Woods after he first stormed on to the golf scene and rose to the top: "There are many putts or many shots where I don't remember hitting. I remember seeing the ball flight. I remember preparing for the shot, pulling the club out of the bag, and once I'm behind the ball, I'm walking into the shot and I don't remember [anything] until I see the ball leave." (YouTube, "Tiger Woods – Getting in The Zone," https://tinyurl.com/tigersez)

Meanwhile you have Jim Nantz or Nick Faldo in the golf show commentary booth, saying, "Look at Tiger's concentration, focus, and determination," but what was Tiger's inner experience? He didn't remember much of what happened. His PFC was offline.

When Bubba Watson won the Masters golf tournament in 2013, reporters asked him after the round what his game plan was on the back nine. His reply: "It's amazing. It's a blur, the last nine holes I don't remember anything." (Golf Channel.com, April 9, 2012, https://tinyurl.com/bubbasez)

When Maria Sharapova upset Serena Williams in the 2004 Wimbledon finals, the biggest upset in the history of Wimbledon, they asked her after the match how she did it. Her reply: "I have no idea." (USA Today, June 2004)

Get the point?

Category 3:

The motion felt effortless and the body felt liquid and free. In golf, "I didn't even feel the club or the putter move" type of statements come to mind.

The motor system is composed of three parts, but the real genius of these parts is the cerebellum. The cerebellum does two things. It monitors where the motion is, and where it must be to be successfully completed. And it can self-correct the motion if something misfires. In other words, if you are at the beginning of your dink and you know the paddle is not in a good position, if you have accessed the correct use of the cerebellum, it will liquefy the body enough to redirect the paddle on the way and square it at impact. The ball may not go in a perfect arc, or land in the most challenging place, but it will still be effective and put your opponent on defense.

If you have not accessed the correct fluidization-enhanced use of the cerebellum, you must make a perfect move on the ball, as the body will not benefit from the activation of any self-correcting mechanisms.

So, how many times do even the best pickleball pros in the world put a perfect move on the ball? Not many. Their activated cerebellums smooth out the motion, which is why they are getting paid to pickle.

A good pickleball shot is a transfer of energy from the lower body to the upper body, to the arms, hands, and then to the paddle. At each part during a motion, there are transitions occurring. When the transitions are not smooth, it is simply because the cerebellum is not doing its job. So how important is the cerebellum in a pickleball shot? Essentially it will determine how far you go in the game. The buck stops there.

Chapter 1— To Flow or Not to Flow

You step on the pickleball court. People are laughing and joking, but somehow you are not so much a part of it today. You are calm. You play these guys every week. The game starts and you are just in some kind of zone. You can't miss. Your dinks are working great. At the kitchen line you get everything. People start saying "Wow you are on fire today." You're glad to hear it, but you don't feel fired up — you are just alert and engaged, and it's all working. Suddenly it's your serve at 10-3-2, and you place the serve deep in the corner, and that's it, no return and it's game over. You get compliments and high-fives. Great day! Let's call it Day 1.

The next time you play, everyone's chatting as you arrive, and you wonder if you'll have another great day. You warm up as usual and you decide to hit even harder and go for the corners. The game starts but you can't seem to act in accord with your plan. The ball doesn't seem to come off your paddle right, especially in comparison to last week. You miss an easy ball mid-court on your way to the kitchen line. Your dinks fall short. Your partner seems to blow easy shots. You get an easy putaway and crank it straight into the net. Your third shot drop seems to be on vacation, morphing into an easy shot for the other team. Let's face it, you are no good at pickleball today. Day 2.

If you are a regular pickleball player you have probably had days like both.

So, what is it that supports the first type of experience rather than the second? How can we set up the conditions so that you have Day 1 type days as opposed to that pesky Day 2 flavor?

The Day 1 experience has several names: the zone, a flow state, in a groove, etc. In this book we call it the Fluid Motion Factor or FMF. We obviously prefer this sort of experience, but most people are resigned to having it now and then, as a serendipitous gift from the Pickleball gods (here we imagine some sparkly green creatures with yellow wings and a mischievous, slightly crazed look in their eyes).

But the purpose of this book is to open the door to a world where you can have a Day 1 experience on demand, just by understanding how all this works in the brain and applying some techniques to activate the zone/flow state/Fluid Motion Factor on demand.

Chapter 2: What Is Fluid Motion?

Some people talk about the zone. We can call it that, though here we typically describe it as the Fluid Motion Factor, or Fluid Motion. Fluid Motion is that strange and beautiful place athletes talk about as if it were a mythical land. A zone, a current, an effortless glide. One moment you're struggling, trying, overthinking. Then suddenly something shifts: the racket moves by itself, the ball feels magnetically attracted to your paddle, and points unfold with a kind of inevitability.

What makes Fluid Motion so slippery is that it arrives only when you stop chasing it. You can't brute force your way in. The prefrontal cortex (PFC) — that chatterbox narrator in your head — wants to command, direct, critique. It tries to drive the bus. But in flow, the PFC takes the back seat, letting deeper systems of the brain and body handle the ride.

We'll go into detail on the PFC and the other, deeper, more Fluid Motion-flavored systems soon, but for now, just consider that this book is about clearing the way for them to take the wheel on every shot. Not through mystical spells or mechanical drills, but by learning how to stop interfering.

We'll explain how with Fluid Motion your body's natural intelligence is operating without the drag of self-consciousness. It's not just a state of peak performance: it's a state of freedom.

Think of it this way: Fluid Motion is less about trying, and more about getting out of your own way.

For a pickleball player, this methodology is especially timely. Most pickleball players have no lack of focus, no lack of urgency and desire. They are deeply focused and intense. They are highly attached to doing well and winning. In fact, the sport is very fast moving, and many lost points result simply because one party couldn't react fast enough. A pickleball point typically starts with what appears to be a mild underhand serve, but it quickly escalates into what can be described as an emergency, often out of control by either team.

In fact, the hyperalert, hyper focused nature of pickleball play can itself become a problem. For some people, playing pickleball is like swatting flies — they think that reacting as fast as possible is the path to success. And that's because the ball often comes their way too fast — beyond their ability to react. They simply cannot process the situation fast enough to respond effectively. So, they think that what they need to do is speed up everywhere, all the time.

We'll clarify why that is not the answer, soon.

In this book we will discuss why that scenario is aggravated by players who are using their mind in the wrong way, how playing pickleball in one way adds a significant amount of time to their shots, measured in milliseconds.

We offer a path to faster, more effective pickleball play. We offer a way out of what could be called pickleball prison, where you try, you practice, you intensely focus, and you swear under your breath when you (or your partner) miss, and you wonder how you can get better. And how you can find your way back to the joy, the hilarity, the camaraderie, and the happiness that you first had playing this new and fascinating sport.

We'll discuss the science, anatomy, psychology, and even the poetic perspectives of the Fluid Motion Factor, and we think you'll enjoy every point, even if the score sometimes is 7-11-2.

Chapter 3: The Hips Don't Lie (but your brain might be a factor)

To understand this on a more granular level, we benefit by looking at some of the cognitive processes that are engaged in playing any sport, and in this case, specifically pickleball.

To start with, we are going to discuss the physiological elements that matter most for Fluid Motion: the prefrontal cortex, the pons, the cerebellum, the basal ganglia, and the amygdala. Plus proprioception. Each one has a distinct role, and together they form the orchestra of effortless play.

Prefrontal Cortex (PFC): In everyday life, the PFC is the brain's CEO — analyzing, planning, and judging.

Pons: The pons is the brain's bridge — relaying signals from the cortex down to the cerebellum.

Cerebellum: The cerebellum is the master fine tuner. It calibrates timing, balance, and precision in microseconds — things no conscious mind could manage.

Basal Ganglia: Think of the basal ganglia as your personal playbook. It stores the motor patterns you've repeated thousands of times.

Amygdala: The amygdala can hijack attention — flooding your system with anxiety. Managed well, it transforms pressure into heightened awareness, helping you play at your sharpest.

Proprioception is your body's ability to sense its own position and movement in space, without needing to look. Proprioception is nearly instantaneous, delivering continuous updates in real time (tens of milliseconds), so the cerebellum and basal ganglia can keep the paddle aligned.

Together, all these systems cut reaction time from "too late" to "just in time," making fast rallies playable. When they harmonize, pickleball feels less like struggle and more like music — a rally that plays itself through you.

The Crazy Thing

To perform an action, you don't really need the PFC and the pons engaged. But you always need the cerebellum and the basal ganglia. The latter two are superfast, faster than the incoming ball, in almost all cases. The PFC and the pons are extra unneeded baggage that simply slow you down.

The Big Boss — He means well, but...

From the Fluid Motion Factor perspective, the prefrontal cortex (the "Boss") is at its best when it's quietly occupied with something other than supervisory remarks and commands. That's why we recommend focusing on certain in-play techniques (called Fluid Cues) that give that bossy PFC something harmless to do, freeing the silent, under the radar systems to run the show. In this way, the PFC shifts from commander to silent, amused observer.

Okay, so here's some nerdy stuff to clarify the situation:

Why the Prefrontal Cortex Is Too Slow for Pickleball

On paper, the prefrontal cortex is brilliant. It analyzes, plans, and strategizes. But in live play, it's the slowest runner in the race.

A prefrontal cortex-driven decision typically takes about 200 to 500 milliseconds, and its signals must also be routed through the pons to the cerebellum, where another 20 to 30 milliseconds are added.

By contrast, the cerebellum and basal ganglia operate at dramatically faster timescales. The cerebellum fine-tunes timing and coordination in tens of milliseconds — essentially instantaneous compared to the PFC — and the basal ganglia can trigger stored motor programs in around 100 milliseconds or less. This means that when proprioceptive input drives play (more on proprioception later), the cerebellum and basal ganglia are fast enough to keep pace with any shot on the court, from lightning-quick kitchen exchanges to deeper baseline rallies, while the PFC on its own is simply too slow.

Let's look at some paddle-to-paddle shot flight times for an average pickleball player, in milliseconds.

Kitchen line to kitchen line	320
Kitchen line to baseline	565
Baseline to baseline	667
Soft dink, kitchen	1400

If you activate the PFC, you are automatically adding 220 to 530 milliseconds to every one of those shots.

You don't need those to function smoothly and effectively, so in effect you have wasted a lot of time putting them in the game.

But you do need 120 milliseconds for the cerebellum and the basal ganglia to fire. If you are running those two, plus the big slow guy, you will need 340 to 650 milliseconds to execute a shot effectively.

Based on the figures above, only a baseline-to-baseline shot is certain to give you that much time.

What that means is simple: at the kitchen line, and a lot of other times, most fast exchanges are faster than your prefrontal cortex can consciously decide what to do. In other words, by the time your PFC boss says "Hit it back" or "Hit it that way" the point is already over. Which is why we lean on the body's silent systems — cerebellum, basal ganglia, and proprioception — to let the rally play itself. It's not just physics; it's Fluid Motion, a.k.a. Pickle Juice.

A word to the computer savvy: the PFC's style of processing is serial, not parallel. It handles about 20 to 40 bits of information per second, compared to the cerebellum and basal ganglia, which can manage millions of motor adjustments per second simultaneously.

This mismatch in speed explains why conscious control feels clumsy and slow in a fast rally. The PFC is superb at planning strategy between points, but in the live fire of most exchanges, while he may be the boss, he simply cannot keep up.

That's why the Fluid Motion Factor doesn't try to make the PFC boss play faster. Instead, it gently occupies the big guy with other activities (Fluid Cues; see below) that deepen and quiet his level of activity, so that the body's faster, more automatic systems can run the point.

The DNA Goal: Why the boss butts in

To understand why the boss gets so involved, we need to introduce another major factor at play, which Steven calls the DNA goal.

Every sport has certain goals built into their very DNA. In golf, it's hitting a little ball with a club so that it travels anywhere from hundreds of feet to a few inches to fall into a hole, with the least amount of strokes. In basketball it's a matter of advancing a ball along a floor without carrying it, which means bouncing it, and then getting it to go through a hoop ten feet high.

In pickleball, we have no problem remembering that it would be a good idea to hit the ball in such a way that clears the net, lands inside the opponent's court and, if possible, adds difficulty to our opponent's ability to do the same thing.

This obvious knowledge is essential to the sport, like DNA is to human function. It only becomes a problem when the DNA goal is the dominant focus of the game. When we are entirely focused on an outcome such as the DNA goal, it detracts attention from the processes that are most likely to support accomplishing that goal.

Every athlete has had the thought "We've got to win this point" or "Hit it hard!" But none of this helps to accomplish that. All that does is to wake up and engage the prefrontal cortex.

Now let's say you have a high ball at the kitchen line. Regardless of what is going on in the game — or even in your life — does anyone have to remind you it would be a good idea if you made the shot? No. But the problem occurs when you make the DNA goal the surface goal: "I have to hit this — angled off with pace — and win the point!"

Let's call this Plan Type A. Plan Type A is: The more important the situation, the more focus, concentration, and determination you think is needed.

When you do that, it tends to systematically shut down the Fluid Motion Factor. Why? Because the quickest way to shut down the Fluid Motion Factor is to have more focus, concentration, and determination than necessary. Then you are giving a green light for the PFC to go online and check to see how you are doing with things.

Remember, the PFC is the CEO of the brain. Just like a real CEO, it wants to investigate and see what is happening everywhere. **If you give it the slightest invitation to go online, it will instantly take advantage of that invitation**. Plan Type A sends a handwritten, personally signed invitation for the PFC to go online, analyze everything, and mess things up.

When you played your best pickleball, would you say it was characterized by more intense focus, concentration, and determination? Probably not. It's far more likely or typical that you just played with flow and freedom, and everything just sort of went well. So why would you default to those intense attributes, especially in pressure situations?

You shouldn't. No need to, anymore.

In this book, you will learn Plan Type B. Plan Type B includes several practices or clues that are a much more intelligent plan than Plan Type A. Plan Type B is not our plan — it's nature's plan. It's systematically aligning yourself with how the brain physiology produces Fluid Motion. Because of that, it greatly increases your chances of playing consistent pickleball. Of course you need a certain amount of focus, concentration, and determination to play consistently, but less than you think.

Much less.

The DNA goal is not going to go away. You are not

going to forget it. There is no chance that you are going to start hitting balls everywhere. We just want all that to fade into the background. Still there, but not dominant. We need to bury the DNA goal on our list of priorities. Still on the list, but not #1.

Finally, let's consider a few scenarios whereby the PFC might get activated and bossy. We think some of these may sound familiar:

- Planning a shot in advance
- If a ball comes faster or at a different angle than expected, quickly replanning
- After missing a shot, making a mental note to do it differently next time
- Intense desire to win a point
- Facing intimidation from a "better" player
- Fear of failure
- Fear of success
- Psychological stress moments of any kind

Sound familiar?

You need the Fluid Motion Factor to bypass all this stuff and function effectively in time or even ahead of time.

Pickle Juice.

Chapter 4: Back Story

You may be thinking, "So how do I do it right? How do I give the so-called boss something to do so that I can access the Fluid Motion Factor?" And sure, you can skip this chapter and go straight to the how-to section. But we think you'll enjoy hearing how all this got started.

After Steven Yellen had his own Fluid Motion Factor experience when he was a top player on the University of Pennsylvania tennis team, he thought that it might take a few years to learn how to do it again and package it for others. But it actually took a lifetime of searching and investigation to put it all together.

At some point in his search for answers and methodologies he engaged in conversation with Dr. Fred Travis.

Travis is a neuroscientist who wrote his dissertation on electroencephalogram (EEG) coherence and meditation. Simply put, EEG coherence reflects functional connectivity in the brain, that is, areas of the brain working together as a whole.

Travis, since that dissertation, has become one of the world's experts on the effects of meditation on EEG coherence. He is now the head of the Center for Brain, Consciousness, and Cognition at Maharishi International University, and has co-authored more than seventy papers on the relationship between Transcendental Meditation® and EEG coherence.

For five years in the 1990s he worked closely with the Norwegian Olympic Athletic Committee to study why some athletes consistently medal in international and Olympic games and other athletes, equally skilled, do not.

Along with Dr. Harald Harung from Oslo Metropolitan University, he published these findings in a book, *Excellence Through Mind-Brain Development*. Their book documents that excellence in any field is determined by one factor and one factor alone — the level of mind-brain development. Mind-brain development includes higher brain integration, psychological development, and growth of higher states of consciousness. Everyone intuitively knows it is the mind that separates the great from the not so great, but Travis and Harung were the first to clinically prove it.

Over the years, Steven had the opportunity to spend many hours with Travis. Travis explained in detail how Fluid Motion is produced in all sports and why it shuts down. These conversations allowed Steven to refine his Fluid Motion Factor program.

At one point in their discussions, Dr. Travis revealed an interesting neurophysiological fact about what is called muscle memory: once someone has grooved a motion, such that it can be repeated consistently, muscle memory does not break down. What breaks down is the ability to access what they already own.

Let's repeat that:

Once someone has grooved a motion, such that it can be repeated consistently, muscle memory does not break down. What breaks down is the ability to access what they already own.

On hearing this, Steven immediately realized the enormous implications that this has for athletes in every sport.

For pickleball it means that, if you have been playing for a while, you already know how to hit each shot. You have that information and that capability stored in muscle memory. It's as if you have it in the bank, and all you have to do is go make a withdrawal.

Your potential perfect dink or overhead smash or angled volley is already money in the bank.

But you only have access to your money if you follow the rules of the bank. In a real bank that means you show your ID, sign something, and get your cash. But in the Bank of Pickleball, you need to access your fast and friendly cerebellum, basal ganglia et al., and hit the ball cleanly.

But if for some reason you alerted the boss (PFC) he slows things down, pulls you out of line, and asks for explanations; you never get to the front of the line to get your cash, and the bank window slowly closes while you watch the pickleball floating by.

Chapter 5: The Number Nine

Let's discuss the core tools that reduce interference and allow the body's silent systems to take over. They are the methods that can help disengage the PFC dominance that complicates your body's responses on the pickleball court. We call them Fluid Cues. There are a number of these that Steven has discovered and applied to many sports, but this collection has been assembled for their relevance and applicability to the fast-paced and intricate game of pickleball. You may not need them all. You may not use them all at the same time. The tool is not the important thing, it's the result: the Fluid Motion Factor freeing and opening your game.

Before we get started, let's introduce an analogy for mental activity, in that the mind is something like an ocean. It has an active level of thoughts and intentions, like the waves on the surface. That level can be moving rapidly and dynamically. But it also has deeper and quieter levels. When the mind is quick and surging it has power, but less flexibility. It is committed to a particular task or direction. The settled mind is more flexible — it can flow anywhere, with deep power.

One of the primary Fluid Cues for pickleball leverages this deeper aspect of the mind. To start with, let's consider that the prefrontal cortex likes to stay busy. It's an active element of the mind. If you try to silence it by force, it usually rebels.

That's why Steven sometimes gives players (and the mind) something harmless to chew on — like softly repeating the number 9.

What this means is that when the ball is hit to you, you quietly start counting inside, with a sort of soft version of the number nine. When we say soft, we mean just quiet inside. Not clear. Hardly there. It might even just be sort of an intention to think of the number 9.

What happens in that situation is that you are activating and functioning from a deeper level of the mind. A more dynamic, flexible, and powerful level. That level of mental functioning translates into more superfluid physical function — an ability to make micro-adjustments on the fly, to make last microsecond changes for a more fluid and effective stroke.

You access that level with that soft inner 9, and then as you hit the ball, you can use a sort of long 9. Counting 9 inside provides a gentle task for the PFC, disengaging it from interfering with movement. It's like giving a restless child a coloring book so they settle down. Meanwhile, your deeper systems — cerebellum, basal ganglia, proprioception — handle the real work of playing.

You might ask, why 9? Why not number 7 or the answer to the ultimate question of life, the universe, and everything in *The Hitchhiker's Guide to the Galaxy*? And the answer (42), as in Douglas Adams' book, is that it doesn't matter. Just roll with it, 9 works just fine.

The brilliance of the number 9 technique isn't in the number itself, but in its role as a substitute. By occupying the conscious mind with something meaningless (but deep), you free the body to act meaningfully, in freedom.

Now, admittedly, there is not a lot of time for counting in pickleball. In tennis Steven advises starting the 9 count on every incoming shot, since the court is bigger and players in general have more time. But for pickleball just keep counting nines throughout the point.

You can even use this on the serve, starting the count just as you toss the ball.

This may seem like a trivial thing, but sometimes even doing this in a practice rally opens you up to as pure a zone experience as anything imaginable. Instead of hitting two or three balls followed by a miss, you can experience a dozen pure shots, wonderfully free. Fluid Motion.

Chapter 6: The Pause (it's a short thing)

Another Fluid Cue you can use is "the pause." Just before the hit — the fraction of a second when everything in you wants to lunge — you insert a micro-stillness.

This works perfectly well with the number 9 Fluid Cue we just described. Or you can try it alone.

In fact, you may try one of these cues and then another. Maybe one day you will emphasize one and it won't be working for you, so you move on to another. We are providing these cues as doorways into the Fluid Motion Factor experience. We are not attached to the cues. We just lightly entertain them. The cue is not our goal, the FMF experience is. It's your home, your natural state. We just unlock the door and step in.

This "silence within silence" interrupts the reactive impulse. It gives your deeper systems a moment to align. You don't wait in a heavy way; you simply allow a flicker of stillness, then let the shot unfold.

Players often describe this as uncanny. The ball doesn't feel rushed, even though time hasn't slowed. The pause introduces grace into motion. It is restraint but also release.

Chapter 7: Acknowledge the Ball

Let's consider the intense focus on the ball immortalized by thousands of coaches in the oft-repeated phrase: "eye on the ball."

We are told to focus on the ball, put our attention on the ball, watch the path of the ball, maybe even watch the seams of the ball as it is spinning.

And did we mention keeping your eye on the ball? This intense focus makes lots of sense. But it may not actually be the best advice.

Acknowledging the Ball vs. Focusing on It

Most players are taught to "watch the ball!" — a command that often creates strain. Focus is good, but intense focus narrows vision, tightens the eyes, shoulders, and jaw, and pulls the prefrontal cortex into overdrive: "Track it harder, don't miss, keep your eye glued to it." The result is tension, over-control, and slower reactions.

The Fluid Motion Factor approach reframes the traditional instruction with a lighter cue: "Acknowledge the ball." To acknowledge is to simply notice — a quiet "There it is" — without strain, chasing, or effortful tracking. The ball is accepted as part of the wider visual field, seen but not obsessed over.

This subtle shift has profound effects on the brain and body. The prefrontal cortex relaxes, no longer attempting to micromanage the act of watching. The cerebellum receives a cleaner visual feed, which allows timing to improve because vision is not being forced. The basal ganglia are freed to release stored motor patterns automatically, rather than having strokes constructed step by step in conscious thought. The amygdala, which often floods the body with anxiety in moments of urgency, begins to calm; urgency remains, but panic does not. Finally, proprioception integrates seamlessly, allowing the ball's position to merge with body awareness so that adjustments feel smooth and natural.

Acknowledging the ball, rather than fixating on it, lightens the situation and opens the door for the Fluid Motion Factor experience to emerge. It dissolves the tension of "trying" and lets the body's silent systems step forward. The player stops staring the ball down like prey and instead welcomes it as part of a wider flow.

And in that lightness, the Fluid Motion Factor experience emerges — effortless, responsive, and alive.

In doing this, rather than experiencing the ball as the central point of an emergency, it recedes into importance and takes its place in a much larger process that includes your movement to the ball, your shot, and even the entire space that you are moving in. Without an obsessive focus on the ball you are freed to engage in all the behaviors necessary to play the point. It's freeing and so radically different from what you have been doing that it's as if you are playing an entirely different sport.

That's a Fluid Cue for Pickleball.

But there's more.

Chapter 8: Shrinking Court

One of the most profound insights in this approach is the idea that you should never throw your mind over the net before the ball.

We're going to say that again.

You should never throw your mind over the net before the ball.

This is one of the most recent perspectives that Steven has revealed in his Fluid Motion Factor instruction, and it is deeply transformational. It's a simple concept, but so radically different that it takes some unpacking.

Let's consider this scenario, which is not what we want, but it should sound perfectly normal, at least for now.

You see the ball hit by your opponent. You instantly react and start planning where you intend to hit the ball back. You rush to the ball, focusing intensely on it, trying to put as much force or at least craftiness into hitting the target that you have chosen.

So... doesn't that sound like what you should do? Or even what you have been trying to do for many years?

Maybe so for some people, but not for anyone trained in the Fluid Motion Factor system.

What happens when you do that kind of thing is that your intense, brilliant, focused plan for your shot interferes with the actual performance of the shot. You have defaulted to the DNA goal, which is to hit the ball in a difficult place for your opponent. Your intense focus on that goal is as if a loudspeaker were going off in your head, broadcast from the PFC: "Hit it there! Hit it there! Hit it there!"

All that noise gets in the way of the Fluid Motion Factor. Of course, we care about where the other person is standing. Of course, we are interested in hitting the ball in some place that will be difficult for them to handle.

And we do that not so much out of malevolence, but because it is our job to challenge them, to invite them to deploy and display what all their training and skill can accomplish. As athletes we need each other to rise to higher levels of excellence.

But we don't need to spend the entire shot obsessing about those DNA goals. When the ball is hit to us we have a snapshot of where our opponent is, and we instantly know where we'd like to hit it. That DNA goal isn't going to disappear in the fraction of a second that it may take for the ball to get to us. What needs our attention is the ball itself.

This is the origin of the concept of the shrinking court. When the ball is on the far baseline and about to be hit, you have the entire court in your awareness. But after the ball is hit we suggest that you imagine that the court is getting smaller as the ball gets closer to you. When you are about to hit, the only thing that concerns you is the tiny space between you and the ball.

You still have the DNA goal of where to hit the ball stored in memory. You haven't forgotten it — you are going to act on that information. But your immediate attention is right there in the "now" moment of making contact.

This has an amazing effect in several areas. First of all, there is a sort of zen-like calm as you meet the ball. Secondly, your vision and awareness of the ball is heightened.

Racket sports coaches repeatedly advise players to watch the ball. But it is amazing how infrequently and inadequately that advice is followed in practice.

And that is because the mind operates in a time zone that is way faster than physical reality.

Once a normal player has latched on to the DNA goal of hitting the ball to a certain spot on the court, that intent takes over the action, affecting even their vision. What typically happens is that the player "checks in" on the ball but does not really watch it all the way to the paddle. The vision gets a little hazy as the ball gets closer, and many times their eyes start drifting toward their target.

In that case, the DNA goal of hitting the target has upstaged the actual process of hitting the ball. They are no longer paying attention to hitting the ball. Then let's just suppose that, despite that, they do hit the ball. Then their eyes are riveted on where the ball is going. But that means that between taking their eye off the ball on the shot and obsessing over where it is going, there has been almost no attention on the actual moment of contact.

Let's contrast this with an observation made of a famous player in pickleball's (older) sister sport, tennis. Roger Federer has been documented many times with photos taken at the actual moment that he hits the ball, and just after, and he is still watching the location of his hit even after he has made contact. This is termed "the Federer Gaze." It's a wonderful behavior to emulate. For Roger, the court has shrunk to a few inches. He is not planning and obsessing about where to hit. He isn't worried about where the ball will go. He knows that unless he pays attention to the ball, he is compromising his ability to accomplish the DNA goal, so he focuses on the task at hand.

In Fluid Motion Factor pickleball, we don't worry about the DNA goal. We know it's there. We don't get ahead of the process, and we are not obsessed with the result; we just have our silent attention on the ball and then the court gets smaller until our entire focus rests only where the ball meets our paddle.

When you do this, you aren't distracted by possibilities: not where the opponent might send the ball, not the score, not the plan. You are fully present with the one shot that exists now. The court shrinks to the size of a single ball.

This local focus produces a paradoxical effect: the less you think about the "big picture," the more naturally your body responds to it. By narrowing attention, you paradoxically expand your freedom.

As a player, some people are constantly surveying the opposing player and their court for openings where they can hit the ball. They are obsessed with winning the point and are waiting for those openings. This hyper-alertness naturally engages the PFC and this vigilant agenda colors their game to the extent that they are known for over-hitting and "going for too much" on every ball.

Let's contrast this with the patient player, the counterpuncher, who lets the other players exhaust and undercut themselves with aggressive, low-percentage shots.

Practicing the Fluid Motion Factor of keeping your mind on your side of the net during the actual shot, experiencing a shrinking court to the point where it's just you and the ball, gives you the opportunity for aggression, when appropriate, but also the utmost in patience and control.

Chapter 9: Soft Eyes

In researching this book, we discovered a concept that has a lot of history that predates Steven's work and yet is deeply compatible: soft eyes.

This is quite similar to the "acknowledge the ball" cue that we presented earlier, but it is worth considering on its own.

To clarify what this is, in practice, let's consider what hard eyes are, on a pickleball court. With hard eyes you zero in intently on where the ball is hit and you intently follow its entire path to your paddle (subject to the DNA goal problems mentioned earlier).

With soft eyes, you don't tightly focus on the ball but let your vision and focus expand to include the entire visible space in front of you, including the position of the ball as it is hit and as it moves toward you.

Paradoxically, this frees you to hit the ball with both more freedom and more precision.

How to Practice Soft Eyes in Pickleball

Before the serve or return, stand ready, but resist the urge to narrow your gaze onto the ball in your opponent's hand. Instead, let your eyes relax and imagine that you are looking through the court, allowing the entire scene to come into awareness — the net strap, the sidelines, both opponents, even the ceiling or sky depending on whether you are playing indoors or out. As your vision softens, you will notice that your breath and shoulders soften with it.

When the ball is struck, keep your gaze wide. Do not chase the ball with your eyes; instead, trust that it will appear within your panoramic field, the way a bird suddenly enters your view when you are looking at the horizon. Your peripheral vision now begins to work with proprioception, telling your body where to move without the need for micromanagement.

As the ball approaches the contact zone, remain soft until the last heartbeat before impact. At that moment, if you wish, let your eyes briefly stabilize on the ball in a kind of mini "quiet eye." This is not a hard stare, but rather a gentle settling of attention at the point of contact.

During and after the hit, let your vision expand wide again immediately. Notice how your body flows naturally into the next movement without tension. This continuity of Soft Eyes keeps you in rhythm and prevents you from locking up after a mistake.

This concept has been used in martial arts, archery, improv theater, and equestrian arts (see

Sally Swift's *Centered Riding*) and Biofeedback (see Les Fehmi's *The Open-Focus Brain*).

Soft Eyes is, at its heart, a "non-interference" cue. By occupying the prefrontal cortex without issuing commands, it prevents the PFC from micromanaging. The cerebellum benefits from a smoother, global visual feed, which improves timing and makes for more natural contact. The basal ganglia are freed to run established patterns with fewer interruptions. The amygdala calms, so urgency remains without tipping into panic. And proprioception integrates vision and body position, connecting movements. It's all good.

But before we go, let's raise the camera up, yes up, way higher, way up above the pickleball court, way above the city, and come down on a football field.

Now that we're here, let's look at Soft Eyes from a football perspective. And let's talk with Luke Jaicks, who is the D-Backs (defensive backs) whisperer (Coach) at East Texas State A&M (Go Lions!). Luke explains it like this:

> "In zone coverage, you need to have wide vision — you need to know what the quarterback is doing, where he is facing, then if he is looking in a particular area of the field you more or less weave your movement in that direction, and if he looks somewhere else, you as if weave back that

way. At the same time, you need your vision to be wide enough to take in the route being run by receivers. Then when the QB pulls the trigger and passes the ball, you are already there to make the best play to either break up the play or intercept."

So... Soft Eyes has value, even when you are carrying 20 pounds of equipment.

Chapter 10: Fearless Pickle

So, we've talked about how to access the Fluid Motion Factor.

Everyone who has gone through the Fluid Motion Factor program, either in person or online, knows that somehow, one way or the other, the Fluid Motion Factor must be accessed. This makes sense, as it is a universal process that produces a fluid, smooth, and powerful shot for everyone. And they all learn a simple, repeatable way to access it. The program has gone through many iterations over the years, in multiple sports.

When you work with better players, it always elevates your own teaching, and as the adage says, often the teacher learns more than the student. This was certainly my case. But after working with some very good players, we were confused. As we mentioned, everyone who went through the program was convinced they must access FMF, and everyone was satisfied they learned a simple way to do that.

But the program hit a wall. Some very talented players could do the program in a practice match, but in a tournament situation, they were struggling. We were confused by this. If they were sold out to the program, which they were, and they knew how to do the program correctly, which they did, why couldn't they do it successfully in a tournament? After all, the program doesn't teach you to do something; it teaches you to do less, until it feels like you are doing nothing. Why couldn't someone do that on demand?

After some reflection, we came up with the answer in one word.

Fear.

As tennis players who have competed our whole lives in tennis, and are still competing, we know this is what shuts you down when you play. Fear. We know players who could do well on the court in practice matches, but can't in competitive rounds, due to experiencing fear. Most athletes have fear to a certain extent, but when it crosses a threshold, it will prevent the cerebellum from doing its job.

And it's there in pickleball as well.

Fear takes many forms in pickleball, since, despite its origins as a somewhat hilarious backyard game, it has evolved into an intensely competitive weekly and even daily sport with pro players and television coverage. You may fear losing, or looking stupid, uncoordinated, and incompetent. You may fear letting your partner down (who you often just met). You may fear not being invited back into the "good" group. You may have fear even in the heat of a point because you want to win it so badly that your fear starts shouting in your head "Don't miss!" and you of course do.

Fear doesn't show up because you are having a bad day. There is always a deeper reason why you are experiencing it. And the origin is not on the surface but rather buried deep within the mind. After some reflection, we came up with five origins of fear:

1. Fear of failure
2. Fear of success
3. Playing for someone else
4. Not worthy
5. Not comfortable in one's own skin

Let's look at each of these from a pickleball perspective.

FEAR OF FAILURE

If you are no good with failure, if you can't really handle it, if it stops you cold, you are probably not playing pickleball, because there are so many ways to fail in pickleball, and 90% of them can make you doubt your competence, coordination, judgment, attention span, or your ability to do the simplest thing. In fact, pickleball offers so many opportunities to completely miss the ball, fail to lift it two inches higher, pop it up into your opponent's easiest shot zone, or hit it long, short, wide, etc., that it will sometimes feel like you failed a zillion times in a single morning.

Add to that a ravenously aggressive opponent only 5 feet tall weighing 90 pounds standing 14 feet away who is already planning to hit the ball in the most challenging spot possible even if that means directly into your chest, and you have an omnipresent opportunity to fail with a capital F.

So, there is no need to fear failure in pickleball. Fear is a worry about something that might happen. In pickleball, it is already happening. Of course, you might fear that it will happen again soon, so there's that.

What we need is a different value system entirely that does not evaluate your success in controlling the game beyond what is reasonably under your control. What we need is a system of self-evaluation that concerns itself with optimizing spontaneous performance rather than intellectual control.

As we have discussed, the prefrontal cortex is the home of self-image, of self-judgment. It's only with an active PFC that you have any concept of failure. With the PFC offline, you allow the cerebellum and basal ganglia to engage at their most supreme level, and if the other person wins the point, you are operating from the most successful possible level, and there is both a major win and major joy in that action, even if the other party wins the point.

We accept that our opponents will win points. That need not create fear. Pickleball operates at time scales that exceed human competence, even with only the cerebellum and basal ganglia in play. We don't fear losing points, because our win is within. And with that inner win, we naturally win more points, but as a by-product of our inner agenda.

In fact, winning the point is not actually the point, at the end of the day. Playing your best without internal noise with the support of the Fluid Motion Factor is the real point, means, and goal of a great pickleball experience. Points will come and go, but the enjoyment of your own amazing, spontaneous excellence is what you take home.

FEAR OF SUCCESS

It seems contradictory to think that this exists, but it does. Complete success is rare. Moving into success requires change. Success can mean leaving a group of friends behind. Sometimes major success invites jealousy and even ostracism from a group of average performers. Then you must evaluate, "Do I want to be successful or do I want friends?" A lot depends on how you define success. Some people only accept being the best at everything, and it is a reality that such a perspective can be off-putting to one's peers.

From the perspective of this book, success is defined internally, in that you have been given a method to successfully channel your own capabilities to the maximum degree. That success does not take away from anyone else's success. It just means that you will gift your opponents the best possible version of yourself. If you are playing with or against people who want you to fail, who want you to be injured, incapable, and have a bad day so that they can win, then the fear you need to recover from is the one you may have in wondering how you can replace those opponents with some healthier people.

PLAYING FOR SOMEONE ELSE

There's an anecdote from Steven about this one.

I worked with a D1 golf team in Florida. They liked the program, especially the best player on the team. Fast-forward a year later and I am at an LPGA tournament watching one of my players, we'll call her Selena, and I then see that top player from a distance and I go up to her and ask her how she is doing. "Selena" was excited to see me and said, "Fine." I said "great!" and then asked her if she was still using the program and she said "Of course, but I am not getting the success I want." I said, "Oh really, do you want to talk about it?" Her response: "Yes!"

We found a quiet area and sat down. I could see she had a lot on her mind and asked her to tell me what was going on. She said she really enjoyed the program but had some challenges. I asked her what kind of challenges. She said she could access FMF on the range and in practice rounds but was having difficulty accessing it as consistently as she would like in tournaments.

Got it.

Just to make her comfortable, because I knew what was coming down the line, I repeated what she told me. "So, you can access it on the range, in practice rounds, but not as well as you would like in tournaments." She said yes, that is exactly the situation. I then asked her if she wanted to understand the problem from a deeper level, because I knew we were about to expose an open wound.

She quickly said, "Yes, I want to understand what is going on."

So, I asked her the million-dollar question: "Where does the fear come from?"

She froze for a split second but quickly recovered. I could tell she was going into a deep, self-reflective mode. What I had asked her was perhaps the most penetrating and personal question you can ask an athlete, as it lays open one's soul. It is not like I knew her all my life; I didn't. Or that we had deep discussions about things in the past; we hadn't. But I felt she trusted me, so I took a chance and asked her.

She said, "I don't know."

I said, "Why don't you think about it and when you are ready, give me a call and we can discuss it."

I then gave her a warm hug and said goodbye.

The next day I got a call from her. I was surprised.

She said, "I have been thinking about our discussion, and I want to tell you a story and see what you think. When I was growing up in my country, I was the best 10-year-old player. Nobody could beat me. I even beat players who are now on the LPGA tour. But for some reason, I started playing poorly and the players I used to beat started beating me.

"One day a group of mothers of the kids I was playing with came up to me and said, 'You are not playing the way you used to play. Maybe you would be happier in another sport?'"

I told her to stop right there.

"So, you are playing now, to show these mothers, whom you probably don't even remember, that you are good enough to compete and win."

She said, "Exactly."

The memory of that stinging statement that went deeply into the mind, heart, and soul of a 10-year-old, so many years ago, was still pulsating. Even after all these years, she was playing for someone else, and not herself.

In the next three tournaments, she had a top 5, a top 10 and a top 20 finish.

If someone can't access FMF, whether they believe in FMF or even know about FMF, it is because of a block. If the mind can only settle down to a certain level and then it hits a block, you will not be able to create the silent, abstract, holistic environment necessary for the subtle processes in the mind to sync the swing.

Because of that, you may never reach your potential, unless that block is removed. It doesn't matter how much you practice, how many lessons you take, or what you work on in your game, that block has to be removed. For her, it just took one conversation. For most it is not that easy, as you will now hear.

NOT WORTHY

Another story from Steven.

I worked with a professional golfer who has long since retired and moved onto another role in the industry. He heard about my program through David Leadbetter. This player was very talented, world class in every aspect. But after meteoric success, he stopped winning. Everyone was surprised, most especially himself.

One day we were playing on his home course. The course was empty. No one behind and no one in front, so we could take our time on every hole. We got to a short par four, and he teed it up, telling me he wanted to hit a high draw. First ball, no high draw. Second ball, no high draw. Third ball, no high draw.

I was puzzled. I asked him, "What's going on?"

He paused for a second, as if he were debating whether to say what was on his mind. I felt he was either going to tell me something revealing or just not reply. He answered: "After a while in my career, someone I deeply admired, a real legend in the game, started saying that I was the best ball striker he had seen since Hogan." And then he went silent, as he wanted both of us to reflect on what that meant.

I said, "So now every time you tee it up, you are trying to prove his statement correct."

Almost under his breath, he said, "Yes." It was almost a surreal admission of the frustration he had felt for so many years and finally was able to admit to someone.

There were other reasons his career faltered. He tried to change his swing too many times, but certainly the almost unconscious desire to prove to someone he deeply admired that what they said about him was correct, played a significant role. He was not playing for himself. He was playing for someone else. As a result, there was a block to accessing FMF. His mind could only settle down to a certain level, so his swing could only be synced to a certain level.

All of us have many levels; we are all complicated to a certain degree. But if you are an accountant or a teacher, you can hide those complications and still have a successful career. You may not be ideal all the time in your work, but you can still have a career.

As a professional athlete, you can't hide. Those complications will be revealed in your performance that day, and the next day when your results are published in the newspaper, and they may cost you your career. There is no place to hide, especially on the back nine on Sunday.

I think, and of course it is only my opinion, that 90 percent of the players on any of the major sports in the world, do not break through, not because of lack of skills, but because of the blocks in accessing deeper levels of silence under pressure. This has nothing to do with the specifics of each sport.

This has to do with life.

What do you do? You know if this applies to you. Well, it's your challenge in life, because if you were blessed with high levels of talent in pickleball and fail to reach your potential, it's a frustrating feeling that may follow you for a long time.

NOT COMFORTABLE IN ONE'S OWN SKIN

Here are our suggestions for being as kind to yourself as possible. Just a few little things.

- Change your diet
- Eat organic food as much as possible
- Eat as little meat as possible
- Eat less fish and chicken, if you can
- Eat less sugar
- Eat more fruits, vegetables, and nuts
- Drink more water
- Avoid fast food and leftovers
- Don't eat too late at night
- Sit for five minutes after eating, so food can be properly digested

Diet is crucial in making the mind stronger and allowing you to cut through blocks and access deeper levels of silence when you play.

Got all that?

Also: consider learning Transcendental Meditation. Both of us have been meditating regularly for 45+ years. We meditate twenty minutes twice a day, morning and evening. It is the single most important decision in our lives because it affects all areas of life.

And, yes, it can help your pickleball game. It will allow you to effortlessly culture more silence in your mind, on and off the court. (More on this in the Appendices.)

On the mental side, start believing in yourself more. Don't doubt your abilities. Doubt kills. Forget what other people say about you or your game. Create your own environment.

Consider closing the book on fixing your shots. That's a big one, so let's say it again (in detail):

Consider closing the book on fixing, upgrading, tweaking, and trying out one more thing that you saw on YouTube on your shots.

Ask yourself: how many years do you want to work on that shot of yours? Is the answer really in the details? When will it be done? Do you really want to be on an eternal quest? If you ask yourself whether you could access what you already know on a consistent basis, would you be satisfied? If you answer yes, then my suggestion is to spend the rest of your pickleball career doing exactly that. It may be the best Pickle decision you ever made.

There will of course still be challenges. Life on every level has challenges. We are here to grow, to learn, to gain wisdom and confidence. For most, this growth takes place in a personal space. For pickleball players, it usually takes place in a public space. You are exposed as an athlete. The world at large sees how you are doing in the classroom of life. You can't hide.

In an office, there is always a place to hide. That is why successful athletes are to be admired, because in front of all their peers, they are showing you how free they can be, when for most, that freedom would not be there.

Perhaps this is why we admire the superstar athlete so much. Both the athlete and the audience, without acknowledging it, know that the ever-present fear that we all have as human beings has been transcended and someone has broken free from it and performed in a spectacular manner that elevates us all. Instantly, they become our role models, regardless of our profession, and inspire us to also be free from fear in our lives. And that is why they are probably worth every penny of all the millions or tens of millions they earn.

When you start going through the program, you are beginning on a journey toward simplicity. It is a journey of self-discovery. You will start being your own teacher. You will learn more about yourself and your capabilities on court. You will be exploring different dimensions about yourself and your game. You will go in and out of using the program correctly.

This is inevitable for everyone as it doesn't matter how many times you tell somebody that they can't own the program or that it's a pattern-less pattern;

the mind is wired such that it wants to go against these concepts.

So be patient with yourself. Be easy with yourself. If you do that, you will be consistent and of course enjoy the game more. Even better than winning is enjoyment of the game. The ability to have freedom and not be a prisoner of the very strict boundaries that pickleball offers is a beautiful, beautiful feeling and stays with you far longer than the score you put on the scorecard. It could affect other areas of your life, as there are boundaries everywhere in our lives. Transcending those boundaries is very much what life is all about.

We'll share one more of our favorite stories. It clearly illustrates the power of our minds. Jimmy Walker was a talented golfer but wasn't having much success. He and others knew he had the talent to make it, but the results weren't there. He got hold of Butch Harmon's number and texted him, asking if he would be willing to work with him. No response. A couple of months later, he texted again.

Again, no response.

Finally, Jimmy's wife took the phone and texted, saying "Butch, we have texted you twice with no response, so please tell us one way or the other whether you will work with Jimmy, so we can plan our lives accordingly."

Five minutes later, Butch texted back, apologized for not responding earlier, and said he knew about Jimmy's talent and would be delighted to work with him.

The rest is history. Jimmy won three times in his first eight PGA tournaments in 2014, right after working with Butch. In 2019, one of the golf magazines interviewed him about his success and having Butch as his coach. They of course asked him about the swing changes Butch made. Jimmy said we didn't do anything with my swing. He told me I had the talent to win on tour and that was all I needed to hear.

What a brilliant and poignant story. We are all probably much better than we think we are.

But let's bring all this back to pickleball.

Let's take another look at two kinds of players.

The first player is 99% of all players. Virtually everybody who hasn't read this book. Are they living in fear? In essence, yes. And that's because they have a particular goal: they want to win. They are gathering all their forces to avoid the dreaded loss. That intense desire creates someone who is engaging all their intellect, willpower, physical skill, memory, tactical abilities, and personal dominance to overcome the opponent. And normally we celebrate the successful deployment of all that intensity on court. In some ways, we idealize the athlete who does all that.

However, there is another sort of athlete who we revere even more, and that is the player who retains a sense of play, or improvisation, of creativity and joy, even with millions of dollars on the line.

Sport can be intense, but we often forget that it is intrinsically play.

The Fluid Motion Factor player wants to win as well. That is one of the DNA goals in all sports. That is not going to go away. We could say that the goal of the FMF athlete is fundamentally different from the 99% because his or her goal is to have the FMF experience. But even that is a bit misleading, because any time you have a goal, it implies that you do not yet have what you are seeking.

The Fluid Motion Factor experience is not exactly a goal, a state of doing, or an achievement — it is more like a state of being, an internal approach. You don't exactly achieve it, you function from that level to whatever degree possible. You activate what you already have. You access the shots that you already own, at will.

In pickleball the fear-based player is living in a state of hyper-alertness and tactical planning. They have a hair trigger slam ready to go if they get a high ball at the kitchen line. They are thinking all the time about the cool shot they want to hit. When the ball comes to them, they must make a split-second decision whether to slam it or dink. They are deeply disappointed when their slam goes long or in the net. Or when their dink is too high or low. They are concerned about how good the other team is and they feel that they need to try harder. They worry that their partner will blow it. They may win, but on some level, they are exhausted by the stress of the whole thing, either way.

The FMF player is virtually on another pickleball planet. Their body feels liquid and free. They are not thinking very much. They are quietly present for every ball. Instead of experiencing pickleball as a series of high-pressure shots, they experience it as a series of peaceful gaps punctuated by deft and effective shots. They have all kinds of time because they are experiencing time normally, not as a series of rushed, inattentive, in-between moments interspersed with important, intense shot moments.

In fact, great pickleball players have a "reset" shot where they slow down the game in situations such as a shootout at the kitchen line. A shootout is really a crapshoot — no one is in control and therefore anyone could win or lose the point, regardless of skillset. Great players exit that risk-filled frenzy and rebuild the point with a soft dink to the opposing kitchen line.

The Fluid Motion Factor pickleball player has as if a reset on every shot.

When you operate from deep silence and awareness, more of your capabilities become available. More shot possibilities open. You can create variety, nuance, and challenging surprises because you are not simply responding without choice to the previous shot.

It's really a different game entirely. And more likely a winning one, though the win is a by-product of the deeper orientation of the FMF player. The win is within (and often without).

Fearless.

Chapter 11: Fluid Motion Factor in Pickleball Action

The Serve:

When serving in pickleball, it's an ideal time to use one of the FMF Fluid Cues. The serve is one shot in pickleball where you have control of where you make contact. Even so, once you have looked at the positions of your opponents (and probably locked in a DNA goal for your shot — usually deep in the court), experience that moment of silence, witnessing the ball just before making contact. Or you can simply start with a long 9. On the return side, all of the cues apply, but pick just one to use, to keep it simple.

Here we can also mention a general comment that Steven makes, which we haven't presented as a Fluid Cue, but it still has merit, and that is the single word "innocence."

Consider approaching the serve with innocence. Imagine that you have never hit a pickleball before. Treat it as the first time. When you bring that freshness to the serve, to every serve, the serve is not encumbered by expectation and potential judgment and subsequent recriminations. It's a fascinating discovery, where anything can happen. Then that openness leaves you free to succeed or fail, without extra baggage and open to whatever happens and both open to and prepared for how the ball comes back (or not).

You have the ball in hand ready to hit, or you drop it to hit, and you imagine that you have never hit such a ball before. There is a sense of total freedom and possibility. Your shot has no baggage of the past or concern about the future. You are totally present and curious about this strange, silly, and somehow wonderful moment. You hit with authority and purpose and move on to the next moment.

Returning Serve:

On the return side, everything that we have discussed thus far applies. Sure, you split as they hit, and as the ball comes your way, the court gets smaller, and you make contact. It's that simple.

The Dink:

Dinking is where many rallies stall — not because of poor technique, but because of tension. Players try to "place" the ball instead of trusting the shot.

The FMF approach transforms dinking. You don't place the ball; you receive it. You have soft eyes. You are not rushed. You let proprioception — not tight control — decide the angle. Counting nines, pausing, or softening your eyes can all convert a stiff dink into a fluid one.

The irony is that when you stop trying to look clever or dominate, you play with elegance and are more effective.

Transitions:

Moving from the baseline to the kitchen is one of the most chaotic moments in pickleball. Balls fly, reflexes fire, errors multiply. Many players panic here.

The FMF invites a different approach. Shrink the court to the next ball only. Pause before each hit. Let soft eyes hold the whole court without strain.

What feels like chaos becomes simply the present moment, repeated. FMF transforms the chaos into rhythm.

Sometimes there are points where we feel more under pressure, due to the score. Pressure is mostly self-generated. The score, the crowd, the meaning we attach to a single point — all of it fuels the amygdala's alarms.

The FMF method shifts the game focus from outcome to process. The cues are tools for this shift. Soft eyes dissolve tunnel vision. Number 9 occupies the critic. The pause and the split step (see Chapter 14)) calm the lunge.

When pressure rises, the temptation is to try harder. FMF whispers: try less, be more.

Every athlete wants to do well. But desire has two faces. One says: I want to play beautifully. The other says: I must not look foolish.

The first motivates and the second sabotages. Beneath the surface, these voices may whisper "I want to be respected. I want to be the best. I don't want to look stupid or weak."

FMF offers a third way: curiosity. What happens if I let the body play? What emerges if I don't force? This curiosity is desire without clinging — energy without fear.

Chapter 12: Patience, the Inner Coach, and the Long View

Athletes often suffer from a merciless "inner coach." It scolds, berates, nitpicks every mistake. If it were a real coach, you'd fire it.

FMF requires a gentler voice. The inner coach becomes a companion, not a tyrant. It accepts that performance is approximate, not exact. You aim for the corner, the ball lands near enough. You miss, and that too is part of play.

You can be surprised by what your body did. Sometimes it's even better and more effective than the DNA goal you had in mind.

We have great hopes for your pickleball games using these cues. Having a zone experience is great, but most people just luck into it, like a door opening into a Shangri-La world where you wander around in wonder but then exit and you can never locate it again. We have given you systematic techniques to access the zone or at least some flavor of the zone, at will.

But let's do our reality check. These are not instant and permanent fixes. Our habits of obsessing over DNA goals are deeply ingrained.

In fact, you will need to practice them every time you play. Even then you will typically find yourself at the end of many points where you completely forgot what we're describing here and started just hammering at the ball with ferocious intent. Many of those moments will be followed by a miss.

The difference, however, will be that you will not berate yourself for missing the shot, you will check in and ask yourself what you can do to get into the silent presence of the Fluid Motion Factor, where you play your best.

Patience is essential. These cues take time to integrate. The frenzy of points will still pull you back. You will fail, forget, tense up. That's fine. FMF play grows not through perfection, but through persistence. Over time, the cues become habit, and habit becomes freedom.

Chapter 13: Flow with a Partner

Pickleball is social. Which means flow doesn't happen in a vacuum. Your partner's energy matters.

Sometimes you'll have a partner who radiates joy, who plays lightly, who celebrates the process as much as the point. FMF is easier together. Other times, your partner is tense, angry, even scolding. Their frustration can yank you out of your zone.

Let's consider two people, Jack and Joe.

Let's start with Jack. What is Jack doing on the court? He is intensely focused. He knows exactly how to hit the ball. He's in the match with both feet and highly focused on hitting planned spots on the court. It's a good plan and he's fully committed. In practice, however, he is constantly disappointed and experiences failure after failure because his shots never go exactly where he had planned, and every miss brings him to an immediate sense of what he did wrong and how he should fix it with this or that tweak.

For example, he may note that when he was pulled way to the forehand side, he hit a shot into the middle of the court, and his opponent hit a shot to his backhand corner and he lost the point. So, he plans that the next time that happens he will hit cross court. But he doesn't get pulled way to the forehand side again for 15 minutes and when that does happen, he forgets his new strategy and makes the same mistake, for which he berates himself all over again.

It's simply not reasonable to miss ball after ball and come up with fixes for each situation that you will remember the next time that situation happens. That's too much mental baggage — it's impractical to remember and deploy each fix in time.

In practice we observe our shots, think of how to hit better, how to recruit more power and spin. But we need to do something entirely different in competition.

What is Joe doing on court? Joe is in a completely different space. He does not see himself as the intellectual guide and supervisor of what's happening on court. He is letting the body play. He has already stored up a wealth of experience, flow, and intelligence in his physiology, and he sees himself as a support to letting that emerge. He is watching the ball, he is getting in position, but he is more aware of the quality of his mental state so that he is not interfering with the flow state of the cerebellar/kinetic/muscular relationship. It's not as easy as it may sound, because the sense of emergency and surprise is insistently present, and he must remember his role, which is not to control, analyze, or critique, just to stay out of the way: present, calm, supportive, enjoying the magical sense of play.

So, putting our two guys to one side, let's remember that yes, we care about the score. Yes, we want to win the point and high-five our partner. But even more than that we want to be fully present in the moment and accept that our shots were as good as possible in terms of how much of the Fluid Motion Factor effect we brought to the situation.

Steven is all about the Fluid Motion Factor; he has enough technique and natural talent to last a lifetime. Paul still works with beginners and watches YouTube videos to see what Ben Johns has to say. But when Paul gets out to play, he usually (hopefully, most of the time) remembers to turn off the technical analysis and let the Flow Motion Factor happen.

But let's consider what it's like to play with Jack. If he loses a point, he bitterly denounces himself. And if his partner misses a shot, he is equally chagrined and often verbally so. For someone who has played for years in the "I've got your back" teamwork environment of doubles in tennis, that's quite a shock. When you miss a shot (without an FMF focus) you are already disappointed. Then if your partner adds a critical comment to the scene that includes both opponents grinning and high-fiving, it can feel like a three-on-1 sports outing.

No fun, in other words.

And if pickleball isn't fun, the entire endeavor is called into question. At least in equestrian sports you have a sense of dignity, even if you fall off the horse, with such an exalted name. But with a name like pickleball, if you aren't having fun, it makes no sense.

So, imagine being on the court focusing on your Fluid Motion Factor agenda with someone like Jack. It's as if you are watching a tiny dog running around chasing its tail, biting the tail and anything else that comes close.

But let's take a moment and consider what it can be like if both you and your partner have the same Fluid Motion Factor agenda. Gone are the eye-rolling looks when you miss, the silent treatment, the extreme celebration on a putaway, and the bitter denunciation of errors. Your partner supports not only you but your calm and focused play.

The other team may agonize and celebrate all they like. But the two of you simply look at each other and smile: "We're doing it, we are playing our best, we are moving like silk through these points and enjoying it all. We are invincible, regardless of the score, because our goal is different. Sure, we hope to win the game, but more importantly we hope to feel the Fluid Motion Factor in action."

And you are.

The trick is to play your own game regardless. Let your cues be the anchor. Shrink the court, pause, soften your eyes — and let your presence be a gift, not a counterattack. Over time, partners may feel your steadiness and soften themselves.

In the dream scenario, all four players are playing with an intimate experience of FMF. The play becomes almost musical, as if the game itself is conducting. That is heaven on earth. Or in a much more modest realm, the size of a pickleball court.

Chapter 14: The Role of Technique

Yes, there is an elephant in the room. You can hear it breathing over in the corner. In fact, for most racket sports, it takes up most of the room and this entire discussion is over in the corner. It's an elephant named Technique.

In starting any sport, yes, it's great to get a lesson. Or more likely, a group of lessons. And in some cases, it's a weekly lesson, maybe to improve or maybe just because the coach is so cute/handsome.

Lessons are valuable for imparting technique. How to hold the paddle, where to stand, how to serve, dink, drive, how to hit an overhead (and when you do, please turn to the side and back up — backing straight up has caused untold numbers of pickleball injuries to wrists and crania).

In addition to real life lessons, there are several tons of YouTube videos out there with the latest info on what to do and how. It's the same in tennis, and probably tiddlywinks. (I checked, and it's a yes.)

So, you get the latest technique, and now you want to try it. You get on the court and start practicing. And that's great, it's a good thing. You are establishing muscle memory. But at some point, we need to use that information without constantly reminding ourselves about it.

That's when the Fluid Motion Factor comes into play.

Technique plays another role in most people's play, and that is in self-analysis. When a player has an intention to hit the ball in a certain way at a certain target, they set up an expectation that their shot will perform as desired. When that doesn't happen (which is much of the time), their mind seeks out an explanation. Typically, one of two internal dialogues results, either "I am a complete idiot and can't do the simplest thing" or "I didn't do (x), and therefore I missed my shot."

In fact, neither of these answers is productive. It certainly adds no energy to the situation to berate yourself. That has no resemblance to fun, which is, after all, one of the main reasons to play any sport with the word pickle built into its identity.

But the other thing, the post shot analysis, in fact subtly distances you from the "now" experience that we treasure, since you are saying, in effect. "I know better than that, I know how to do better than that" and you swear that the next time that situation comes up, you will do it the right way.

But that same situation almost never comes up again, and when it does, you generally don't have time to search your memory banks and deploy that stored intention.

And so, you blow it again, and your self-analysis starts to drift from the I did it wrong conclusion over to the idiocy category.

In the Fluid Motion Factor approach, you are not obsessed with results, you are not concerned about mistakes. There are no mistakes except for allowing yourself to get pulled out into the DNA goal, and even that will happen now and then, and you will be okay with that, if it happens.

There are so many variables in pickleball that are beyond your control. The wind may blow that light ball off course. You may grab the paddle at the wrong angle. Someone may yell on the next court. A pretty or handsome human may walk by (that coach!). And there's always the possibility that your opponent will hit a great shot.

None of that matters in comparison to you having a Fluid Motion experience. We have a phrase for this and it's the following:

The Win is Within.

We still love talking technique. YouTube is full of technical advice for tweaking your shots. Most of it has value. But you need to have two gears, practice and play. In practice you stabilize how and where to hit. You must do repeated actions, or you have nothing stored in muscle memory (i.e. basal ganglia, et al.). But when you play it's high time to switch to FMF. And, lest we forget, a good deal of your practice time should be technique-free, just stabilizing the FMF habit. Maybe most of the time.

Chapter 15: Visiting an Old Friend

Speaking of technique, there is one that we can visit in our FMF context, in addition to that familiar "eye on the ball" phrase, and that is the split step. In case you haven't heard (just getting back from Mars? — wow — welcome back!), a split step is a little hop that you can do just as your opponent hits that ball, or (a bit of refinement) just as they start their swing.

Now that we have explained it, we're going to mention that it is misnamed, in that it is not best to think of it as a hop, but rather as a loading step. To move in any direction, you need to push off from the ground in the desired direction. It's not the hop that gets you going, it's the value of your weight pushing into the ground after the hop that allows you to move quickly to the ball.

So, in fact, we don't want to hop as our opponent hits the ball, we want to land from that hop, ready to go.

Having this intention means that you are aware of what your opponent is doing. In fact, you are as if dancing with them. When they move, you are moving to the optimal position to prepare for their shot, and when they hit you are landing your split (loading) shot ready to move.

This technique element is totally in tune with the Fluid Motion Factor, in several ways. First, timing your actions to your opponent's actions requires a big picture, soft eyes approach. And, by taking a moment to prepare for each shot you break up the process of the point into micro-moments, adding more calm into the situation.

Most points start with a serve, and then chaos ensues. It's our job, if possible, to standardize the chaos, get into position to hit one of our oft-practiced shots, and bring calm and order to the chaos. We are at the same time creating entropy on our opponents' side of the court. By performing actions such as a split step, we have a greater chance to get into a position to do something that we have rehearsed dozens to hundreds of times.

When we don't do a split step, we tend to smear our shots together, and the finish of one shot puts us in a weird position and then we're lunging over there to hit another ball, and soon we're attempting shots that we have never tried before.

So, we split step (load) when we can and give every shot its moment. With the Fluid Motion Factor intact.

Chapter 16: The Paradox of Effortless Mastery

The paradox of a zone experience like this is that the less you try to master it, the more mastery it gives you. Effort pushes it away. Non-effort invites it in.

This doesn't mean laziness. It means intensity without strain, engagement without control. You still practice, still compete, still care. But you care differently — less about outcome, more about presence.

In this way, pickleball becomes a mirror for life. The greatest mastery comes when you stop demanding mastery. Effortless effort is not a contradiction; it is the deepest truth.

On court, we are allowed to dissolve anxiety into trust. Off court, it can be the same: a conversation without self-consciousness, a walk where time disappears, a day lived without clinging to results.

Pickleball is small, but within its lines are all the dramas of life: desire, fear, partnership, chaos, triumph, failure. To play with the FMF method is to rehearse a way of being human — lighter, freer, more attuned.

And so the game becomes more than a game. It

becomes a practice. Something to think about. Or just be.

Chapter 17: How to Add This to Your Game

We've given you some Fluid Cues (above). In the appendices (later) we supply some drills and worksheets. You can use all that, but to be real, all of this is not an instant fix to your pickleball game. Instant improvements, sure, a lot of the time.

But this is a complete 180-degree turn in comparison to most athletic endeavors, which are typically driven by intense competitive focus, with egos, bragging rights, self-image, and sometimes even money on the line.

The habits of intense focus and goal seeking are not going away. The DNA goals are never leaving. They can recede into the background when handled properly, but they can also upstage everything if given even the slightest encouragement.

There will be many times when a point is over, and you realize that you have precluded the experience of Fluid Motion and ended up in Shot Land. Shot Land is that familiar place where you tell yourself what to do and where you get excited about your plan for the ball, sometimes even before your opponent has hit it. All that is tied up with the DNA goal and instantly brings the PFC boss onstage, shouting orders.

Trust us, it will happen repeatedly.

However, unlike the recriminations and self-lecturing you used to do when you missed a shot, your goals have changed to supporting Fluid Motion, and when that happens you will simply chuckle at yourself, pick a Fluid Cue and start over again.

Unleashing Pickle Juice is a practice, not a magic switch. It may take a while to remember it in the heat of the moment, but you can easily come back to it and restart it, until it becomes your new modus operandi.

Going that way leads to both freedom and success. We just want you to have access to what you already own. It's your money, and we want you to be able to spend it freely, when you need it, because after all, you've earned it, and it's functionally unlimited. It's like a catalyst — it makes things happen, but it doesn't get used up in the chemical reaction.

Give it a shot. Several shots. And while you do, we think you'll enjoy the new taste of freedom on court: Pickle Juice.

Appendices — Extra Credit

Appendix I — Drills

Part 1: Drills for silent mastery

Practice usually means repetition. But in Fluid Motion Factor practice, repetition isn't about hammering technique — it's about rehearsing freedom.

Drills for silent mastery are designed not to ingrain more conscious thought, but to let the silent systems play without interference.

- Shrinking Court — Get a basket of balls. Have a partner hit a ball to you from the far baseline and don't try to hit it. Just let it get closer and pass by, while your attention shrinks to only that ball. Then do the same thing and catch the ball in your hitting hand, followed by hitting each ball back, but not toward the feeder. Then take it to the final step and do a very friendly rally with that partner. When you play again, add this cue in.
- Rally with a partner while quietly thinking 9 inside. It doesn't need to be a loud and clear pronunciation. Maybe you only had the intention to say the 9, but it's there

somewhere. Then as you hit the ball, just let a long 9 happen. If it helps, try starting this with the same basket of balls and the progression described in the Shrinking Court cue. When you feel like you have a sense of it, play a game repeating 9 silently, noticing how the chatter quiets.

- Pause for a microsecond before every volley (and other shots). See if the Quiet Eye type cue brings more Zen-like calm into your game. The progression works here, too.
- Have someone serve to you and, as they engage with the ball, maintain the wide vision of soft eyes. Experience the magic of an effortlessly effective focus on the ball in the larger context of the entire visible space. Then try the same thing with one up, one back — one person at the baseline and one at the kitchen line, both where the baseline hitter tries a hand-held third shot drop, and where they smash it at you. Finally, try a series of kitchen line to kitchen line volley exchanges, maintaining soft eyes. If you can, let us know how it goes. We think that you will be amazed (send comments to paul@stokstad.com).

These drills may look ordinary, but their intention is different. You aren't fixing strokes — you're loosening them. The goal is not better mechanics but less interference. Paradoxically, that makes your mechanics better.

Appendix II — Expanded Views

We've mentioned meditation a few times, so it may be of some value to consider how that trend in society is related to what we are talking about. When we discuss meditation, we will be sharing primarily the insights and experiences provided by the Transcendental Meditation program (or TM). We are aware that there are many other techniques, from other traditions, including modern versions such as mindfulness. Even though they are grouped under the one term they are quite distinct in methodology, outcomes, and goals.

Without getting into all that, we're just going to present the perspectives with which we have long familiarity on both a theoretical and experiential level.

One of the most striking parallels between our playfully presented Pickle Juice angle and the discussion of TM has to do with a sort of before and after report.

Many people have reported experiences of higher states of consciousness. You can see several of them in Craig Pearson's book *The Supreme*

Awakening on Amazon. There is no shortage.
Wordsworth had a lot to say on it.

William Wordsworth's great poem *Lines Composed
a Few Miles Above Tintern Abbey* mentions:

"Until, the breath of this corporeal frame
 And even the motion of our human blood
 Almost suspended, we are laid asleep
 In body, and become a living soul:
 While with an eye made quiet by the power
 Of harmony, and the deep power of joy,
 We see into the life of things."

And later, in the same poem, he writes:

"A motion and a spirit, that impels
 All thinking things, all objects of all thought,
 And rolls through all things."

Alfred, Lord Tennyson described profound
spiritual or mystical experiences, very much like
Wordsworth's, in what he called a state of "self-
loss" or "ego-dissolution."

In his memoirs, he recounts:

> "A kind of waking trance I have
> frequently had, quite up from
> boyhood, when I have been all alone.
> This has often come upon me through
> repeating my own name two or three
> times to myself silently, till all at once,

as it were out of the intensity of the
consciousness of individuality, the
individuality itself seemed to dissolve
and fade away into boundless being
— and this not a confused state but
the clearest of the clearest, the surest
of the surest, utterly beyond words —
where death was an almost laughable
impossibility — the loss of
personality seeming no extinction,
but the only true life."

But later in life, Tennyson reflected that those
"waking trances" became rarer as he grew older,
and he expressed regret that he could not summon
them at will.

"It is curious that I sometimes had, when a boy, a
sort of waking trance… but now I hardly ever have
it. I regret that it has passed away."

We could point out many of these, but we don't
have to — Craig Pearson already did it.

The intriguing point here is Tennyson's sense of
regret that he could no longer access that
experience.

So, what does this have to do with Pickle Juice, and
its Fluid Motion Factor technology?

It's directly analogous to the elusive zone experiences that many athletes report. They got into the zone, but they couldn't find it again.

So, what does meditation (specifically TM) have to do with this? It's completely parallel. People have often reported spontaneous experiences of (at least temporary) enlightenment, but are unsure how they got there, how to get back there, and if it can become permanent. So, the promise (and proven deliverable) of the TM technique is the experience of what researchers have called a "wakeful hypometabolic state" or restful alertness. Not asleep but deeply relaxed.

It's a technique for getting there repeatedly, and to grow toward a permanent experience.

You have just read about a similar thing that applies on a smaller but still interesting scale: a technique designed to create an athletic FMF "zone" experience repeatedly.

And there's one more intriguing parallel.

Many people think of meditation as passive, inward, escapist, and impractical. But the TM phenomenon has always been described (and documented) as a sort of deep rest for dynamic activity. Research shows that it improves reaction time, alertness, and autonomic stability.

In fact, it has been that orientation toward enhancing practical life that has made the 20-minute twice-daily practice of TM so popular in the Western world. As teachers we don't recommend meditating all day. The idea is to take a deep dive into inner peace and tranquility and then take it out into activity. By doing that, you start to infuse more of that peaceful energy into your daily life, which is a much bigger accomplishment than feeling great for 40 minutes. That's a more enlightened style of existence, not a short-term vacation.

Similarly, when we talk about Pickle Juice, we really are talking about extra juice. It's not that the Fluid Motion Factor makes you passive and quiet. It makes you calmer, certainly, but present, sharp, alert, and effective. But possibly with less yelling, and off the gloating/agonizing scale.

To pull these two threads together, we should mention that incorporating TM into your life, as an athlete, and specifically as a pickleball player, has a lot of upsides.

There are of course all the intrinsic benefits of increased energy, reduction of stress, and faster reaction times.

But a more subtle fact is that anyone who has experienced the inner silence or "restful alertness" of the TM practice is deeply familiar with stable but energetic inner states both in and outside of meditation. Falling into dynamic inner calm, a Fluid Motion Factor state, is for them a default mode that can be activated with Pickle Juice techniques so that even a shot around the post can be executed with peace and precision.

Bibliography

By Steven Yellin

Steven Yellin — *Simplicity, The Fluid Motion Factor for Golf* (on Amazon)

Sports & Performance Psychology

Tim Gallwey — *The Inner Game of Tennis*
Seminal text on awareness, quieting self-judgment, and letting the body play naturally.

George Leonard — *Mastery*
Explores the mindset of lifelong learning, with aikidō insights on relaxed concentration.

Joan Vickers — *Perception, Cognition, and Decision Training*
Introduces quiet eye research — longer fixations before action — a scientific cousin to soft eyes.

Les Fehmi — *The Open-Focus Brain*
A practical guide to diffuse, panoramic attention — essentially "soft eyes" in neuropsychological terms.

The Soft Eyes Tradition

Sally Swift — *Centered Riding*
Equestrian classic introducing "soft eyes" as a way

to relax body tension and expand awareness — a phrase that migrated into wider somatic and sports practice.

Thomas Crum — *The Magic of Conflict*
Brings aikidō principles (including soft gaze and centering) into conflict resolution and performance.

Alan Watts — *The Way of Zen*
Not directly about sports, but foundational in understanding the "effortless effort" philosophy that informs soft eyes and flow.

Transcendental Meditation (TM) & Consciousness

Maharishi Mahesh Yogi — *Science of Being and Art of Living*
The foundational text on Transcendental Meditation — exploring the mechanics of effortlessness in consciousness.

Dr. Robert Keith Wallace — *The Physiology of Consciousness*
Early scientific studies of TM, including EEG coherence — links nicely to flow-state neuroscience.

Craig Pearson — *The Supreme Awakening: Experiences of Enlightenment Throughout Time — And How You Can Cultivate Them*

Dr. Tony Nader — *Consciousness Is All There Is: How Understanding and Experiencing Consciousness Will Transform Your Life*

Other Influential Works on Flow & Skill

Mihaly Csikszentmihalyi — *Flow: The Psychology of Optimal Experience*
The classic academic exploration of flow states — the psychological backbone to what Steven Yellin calls the Fluid Motion Factor.

Josh Waitzkin — *The Art of Learning*
Chess and martial arts prodigy on how to train for resilience, flow, and creative performance.

Daniel Goleman — *Focus: The Hidden Driver of Excellence*
Explores attention styles (broad, narrow, internal, external) — useful lens on soft vs. quiet eyes.

Acknowledgments (thanks are due)

Books, like rallies, are never played alone.

First, gratitude to the countless pickleball players and partners who gave us live laboratories for testing these ideas — the laughter, the failures, the occasional muttered complaints, and the surprising breakthroughs all became raw material for this book.

As co-authors, we owe much to each other. Steven brought the foundation: the Fluid Motion Factor system, decades of teaching, and the clarity of seeing performance at its deepest level. Paul brought the translation: the stories, the playfulness, and the lived experience of making flow real in the heat of actual pickleball play. Without this partnership, the book would not exist.

To Paul's wife, Risë — Master Pilates teacher and master of seeing what bodies are truly capable of. You reminded us that Fluid Motion isn't just about inner calm, but also about appropriately activated dynamism, i.e. — Pickle Juice. Your suggestion that proprioception be included in the discussion gave the physiological section a broader scope.

To the teachers who shaped us in other fields —
meditation, poetry, improv theater, sport — thank
you for showing that effortlessness is not a trick
but a truth. Both of us have been longtime
practitioners (Paul is a Certified Instructor) of the
Transcendental Meditation program (see tm.org),
and that training underlies much of what we value
in the Fluid Motion Factor experience: that the
mind performs best when effort relaxes and
awareness opens. This perspective also informs
our teaching, since we both know that there is
more to every athlete than meets the eye — even if
we must wake them up to the existence of their
own inner depths and how to access and release it.

We can't effectively convey how transformational
that connection has been for us. When you have
studied and experienced the expansion of
consciousness in depth both academically and
experientially (reading, study, teaching, and a
twice-daily meditation experience) subsequent
discussions of Fluid Motion Factor-enhanced
athletics seem like messages from a familiar
country.

We know what it means to feel fully expanded and
free inside. We are already experiencing the value
of a deep inner field that supports daily success
and enjoyment. And the thought of taking all that
inner peace into the dynamism of athletics is a
natural thing.

About the Authors

Steven Yellin is the creator of the Fluid Motion Factor system, a performance methodology that has helped professional athletes, musicians, executives, and weekend competitors play in the zone more consistently. A former #2 tennis player at Penn State, Steven once scored a match victory over a young but already formidable John McEnroe — proof of both his competitive pedigree and his ability to thrive under pressure.

Even so, his path to the deep investigation that resulted in this technology started with an experience during a tennis challenge match that opened his eyes to an entirely new possibility for effective play. It was an illuminating Fluid Motion type experience, and he has since spent decades studying how the brain and body cooperate in peak performance and in teaching the Fluid Motion Factor to athletes worldwide.

Paul Stokstad is a writer, teacher, poet, and lifelong athlete. With over sixty years on tennis courts, six years on pickleball courts, a background in improv theater, and more than fifty years of daily Transcendental Meditation practice, he brings a playful yet insightful voice to the Fluid Motion Factor system. His teaching background, along with his poetic sensibility, helps translate Steven's method into stories, cues, and reflections that resonate with both the competitor and the casual player.

Paul is also, as we have described, a perfect example of someone who has travelled all the way from analytical control to the experience of the Fluid Motion Factor.

But let's consider that he started with tennis and later entered the world of pickleball. In tennis he had years of habit and analysis to rewire and redirect with the Fluid Motion Factor. But in pickleball he had to start from the ground up, and to be clear, at the beginning there are a lot of differences between the two sports.

Tennis players may laugh at pickleball and think that they will easily dominate in what appears to be a sort of toy game. But what they find is that they are not the only athletes in the mix, since badminton, ping-pong, racquetball, and even volleyball players have also joined the ranks, and other athletes as well. And the slash and burn dominance behaviors of tennis don't necessarily translate effectively to intricate, strategic play punctuated by occasional aggressive explosiveness that is more characteristic of pickleball.

Paul experienced a lot of humbling moments in pickleball when players who could barely run easily dismissed him on court with patience and guile. Even so, once he stabilized his pickleball shots (the dink, the ATP, et al.) he started to establish muscle memory that he could access with the aid of the Fluid Motion factor. And now he is a respectable and reliable force on court, combining the lightning reflexes and shot making of his tennis background with the Fluid Motion Factor-enhanced patience and presence in dinks, volleys and drives.

Together, Steven and Paul combine science and storytelling, precision and play. Steven provides the method, the science, and the decades of competitive and teaching experience. Paul provides the lived journey, the humor, and the language that makes Fluid Motion Factor accessible to all. The result is Pickle Juice — a book that celebrates not only performance, but also presence, joy, and the art of play.

But there's more: the Odd Couple

The story behind the Steven and Paul alliance is a classic master/disciple relationship. It all started with playing tennis together, sometimes singles and sometimes doubles. It is, however, a one-sided relationship, since Steven is a master player, and Paul, despite his certified teaching pro status, is simply not on Steven's level.

It is a singularly illuminating experience to play against Steven, since he doesn't overpower you (although he can on occasion, if it amuses him), he simply puts the ball in the most difficult location for you to respond to. In fact, he recently said that he never tries to put the ball away — he just makes it challenging and waits for you to make an error.

And, considering the type A personality, go for broke style that used to characterize my game, I provided that sort of opportunity to him on a frequent basis.

In fact, in searching my brain for reasons why Steven consented to play with me, and even seemed to really enjoy it, I've concluded that the contrast between his cool-headed Fluid Motion Factor and my prefrontal cortex-driven game was so extreme (and, we could say, more or less a tennis train wreck) that he found it simply hilarious to watch me in action.

It's not that I didn't win points, and even the occasional game, but it seems to have mostly been a sitcom for him, but with tennis shoes, so maybe a "runcom."

But, after the amusement wore off, he finally got serious and began providing the new perspectives that we discuss here — on tennis. I was an extreme case — deeply analytical, weighed down by the sense that my brothers had been state champions, college athletes (#1 and #2 at the University of Iowa), and had played in tournaments with Jimmy Connors and other top players. I felt like I should be that good as well and was not making it. And I was a teaching tennis pro, intellectually observing and analyzing every shot, sometimes before, during, and after.

Steven freed me from all that. And because of that I now listen intently whenever we talk. Now and then he takes me out on the court for a check flight regarding how I'm doing on court. But that's for another book.

Final Notes

A thank-you to Steven — who has shown me that the game within the game is not about control, but about letting go.

And to every partner, opponent, poet, and fellow wanderer who's helped me discover that pickleball, tennis, theater, meditation, and even life itself is really the same game: learning to flow from within.

Calm within the storm,
clarity shapes each motion,
grace becomes the game

— Paul Stokstad

We also offer our thanks to the millions of players who have embraced pickleball with such joy, energy, and enthusiasm. Your laughter on the courts, your willingness to try, fail, and try again, your cheers, rivalries, and friendships — all of it has breathed life into this sport. It is your collective spirit that has transformed pickleball from a Bainbridge Island backyard pastime into a worldwide movement. More than a game, it has become a community, a celebration of play, and a living example of how vitality, humor, and connection can bring us all closer.

And finally, to every reader: thank you for bringing

your curiosity here. May these pages help you discover, as we have, that Fluid Motion isn't just a fleeting state, but the way the game — and life — are meant to be played.

— Steven Yellin and Paul Stokstad

Lagniappe

One more note from Paul: Working with Steven is really something special. We are giving you as much information as we can in a book format. A precious few golfers and a select group of other athletes have experienced working with Steven in person. He has been doing this so long and with such deep focus and insight that he can instantly tell whether you are functioning from the DNA goal level or from the good stuff. You can learn more about accessing that sort of attention at his website, Stevenyellin.com. Long term, we hope to offer videos, weekend retreats, and other formats to help stabilize your Fluid Motion Factor experience, for pickleball, for tennis, golf, and other sports. Stay tuned.

Also: If you have any comments on how the Fluid Motion Factor has affected your pickleball, feel free to share them. Please specify if they are not for publication, otherwise we will assume it's okay to use them with your name in promotions or in subsequent editions of this book. For now, please send them to paul@stokstad.com with only the words Pickle Juice in the subject line.

And, if you liked our book, please help with a review on Amazon using this link:
https://tinyurl.com/picklebookreview